GAUGUIN

SPRING ART BOOKS

By Ronald Alley

SPRING BOOKS · LONDON

ACKNOWLEDGMENTS

The publishers wish to thank the following museums, galleries and collectors for their kind permission to reproduce the paintings in this volume: The Trustees of the Tate Gallery, London (Plate xliii); Courtauld Institute of Art, London (Plates xxxix, xl); National Gallery of Scotland, Edinburgh (Plates ix, xii, xliv); Fitzwilliam Museum, Cambridge (Plate i); Biggins Gallery, London (Plate x); Louvre, Paris (Plates ii, vi, xiv, xv, xxv, xxxiv, xlii); Musée des Beaux-Arts, Lyon (Plate xxxv); Carlsberg Glyptotek, Copenhagen (Plates iii, iv, vii, xxiv); Musées Royaux des Beaux-Arts, Brussels (Plate xvii); Kunstmuseum, Basel (Plates xxix, xxxi); Folkwang Museum, Essen (Plates xlvi, xlvii); National Gallery, Prague (Plate xx); Pushkin Museum, Moscow (Plate xxxvi); Museum of Art, São Paulo (Plate xxxviii); Art Institute of Chicago (Plates xiii, xxii, xxxiii, xxxvii); National Gallery, Washington, D. C. (Plate xviii); Albright Art Gallery, Buffalo (Plate xvi); Cleveland Museum of Art (Plate xlviii); Minneapolis Institute of Art (Plates xxvii, xxviii); Museum of Fine Arts, Boston (Plate xli); Museum of Modern Art, New York (Plate xxxii); The Hon. Michael Astor, London (Plate viii); Sir Robert Adeane, London (Plate xix); Maresco Pearce, Esq., London (Plate xxi); Dr Jacques Körfer, Berne (Plate v); Mr & Mrs Niarchos, Paris (Plates xi, xxvi); Mr & Mrs John Hay Whitney, New York (Plate xxx); Mr Walter P. Chrysler, Jr., New York (Plate xxiii); Mr Nathan Cummings, Chicago (Plate xlv). The paintings reproduced on Plates ii, vi, xiv, xv, xxv, xxxiv — xxxvi, xxxviii, xl, xlv, were photographed by Photographie Giraudon, Paris. The frontispiece, a self-portrait by Gauguin in bronze bas-relief, is reproduced by courtesy of A. S. Teltsch, Esq.

1st Edition 1961
2nd Impression 1963

Published by
SPRING BOOKS
Westbook House • Fulham Broadway • London
© Paul Hamlyn Ltd 1961
Printed in Czechoslovakia
T 1129

Contents

Black-and-white Illustrations

Introduction

Our great interest in Gauguin to-day has come about not only because of the value of his work and its influence on modern art, but also because he had one of the most colourful lives of any artist in the nineteenth century. The impression which we receive from him is of a powerful nature struggling to fulfil its destiny, a man driven by violence to extremes and to self-destruction. On the one hand, the cultured European involved in the most sophisticated art movements of his time; on the other, the man who turned his back on western civilisation in order to become a savage, a Maori.

Paul Gauguin was born in Paris in 1848. His father was a journalist of liberal tendencies, and his mother, Aline Chazel, was the daughter of Flora Tristan, a political speaker and follower of Saint-Simon, of Peruvian-Spanish extraction. Shortly before the *coup d'état* of Louis Napoléon in 1851, the family left for Peru, where Aline had influential relations, the father dying en route. Although they only remained there for four years, it may well be that the boy retained impressions of that strange and remote land which, in later years, stirred his wanderlust, for in 1865 he enlisted in the merchant service and made voyages between Le Havre and South America.

In 1871, however, he left the sea and entered the Bertin bank in Paris as a stockbroker. By 1873 he was in a financial position to marry Mette Gad, a young Danish girl, and in the following years made a very comfortable income. He seems to have begun to paint in 1871, soon after entering the bank, encouraged perhaps by his guardian Gustave Arosa, who owned a fine collection of pictures by Corot, Delacroix, Courbet and the artists of the Barbizon School. Arosa's daughter, Marguerite, herself a painter, gave him instruction in the technique of painting in oils and went with him on Sundays to paint at St Cloud on the outskirts of Paris. At Bertin's he found that another employee, Emile Schuffenecker, had also developed an enthusiastic interest in painting. The two of them soon began to take their hobby so seriously that they went in the evenings to the Atelier Colarossi, one of the *ateliers libres* where artists

7

could work freely without the discipline of the Académie des Beaux-Arts, to draw from the model and receive a certain amount of tuition.

Gauguin's early paintings were in the tradition of Daubigny, Corot, Jongkind and Courbet. Maturing rapidly, he exhibited a landscape at the Salon of 1876, but apparently never mentioned this to Arosa or to his wife.

The turning-point in his career was his meeting with Camille Pissarro, which seems to have taken place about 1875. The two became good friends and Pissarro gave Gauguin a great deal of useful advice; they even worked side by side, painting from the same motif, as Pissarro and Cézanne had done a few years before. With the older artist's encouragement, Gauguin began to form a fine collection of Impressionist paintings, including important works by Cézanne, Pissarro, Degas, Sisley, Guillaumin, Monet and Renoir; he also contributed to the last four Impressionist exhibitions of 1880—86. His works of this period show the typical Impressionist handling and broken colour similar to Pissarro, but without much personal quality. As Gauguin said later of Pissarro: 'He looked at everybody, you say? Why not? Everyone looked at him, too, but denied him. He was one of my masters and I do not deny him.' Gaining confidence, Gauguin began to tackle the human figure, getting his wife Mette and the maid to pose for him, or making studies from one or other of his children.

By all accounts, however, he was still not taken seriously as an artist, and probably himself felt uncertain of his powers. His first true success came when be exhibited *Study of a Nude* (Plate iii) — painted from his maid Justine — at the Impressionist exhibition of 1881 and earned the enthusiastic praise of the naturalist novelist and critic J. K. Huysmans: 'I don't hesitate to state that among the contemporary painters who have depicted the nude, none has yet given so vehement an expression of reality . . .' Gauguin became less modest, more assured; the stock market began to take second place. Nevertheless it came as a complete surprise to his wife when he suddenly announced in 1883 that he had decided to give up his job at the bank at the end of the year and become a full-time painter. About the beginning of January 1884 he moved with his family to Rouen, where he hoped to find a market for his pictures among the wealthy bourgeois, but he met with no success and after three or four months was in a precarious financial position. It was decided that Mette should return to Denmark to try to earn a living by teaching French and by making translations. Gauguin joined her there in December, but unfortunately was soon on bad terms with his wife's relations. Embittered by the hostility of the Gad family and by the failure of his one-man show in Copenhagen — a failure which he attributed partly to intrigue — he returned to Paris about the end of June 1885, leaving his wife behind.

8

The sacrifice of family, security and peace of mind to art had already begun. The successful business man was set on a path which would lead to renunciation of western civilisation, bitter poverty, an early death . . . and artistic greatness. 'I am a great artist . . .' he wrote to Mette later by way of explanation. 'I am a great artist and know it. It is because I know it that I have endured so many sufferings in order to proceed on my way, otherwise I should consider myself a brigand.'

Gauguin was not only influenced by Pissarro. He owned, for instance, at least five paintings by Cézanne including works from the period when Cézanne showed the most pronounced interest in simplification, pattern and the use of almost flat areas of colour surrounded by definite outlines. The influence of Cézanne can be seen in his still life of 1885 reproduced as Plate vi, and more strongly in certain other works of the same period. Afterwards, in 1890, he included the still life from his collection in the background of one of his portraits (Plate xxii), a picture which may be regarded as a kind of homage to Cézanne. He even took a fleeting interest in the innovations of the Neo-impressionists, whose contributions had been the main attraction at the last Impressionist exhibition of 1886, though he soon turned against Neo-impressionism and referred contemptuously to its exponents as 'confetti painters'. He insisted that the juxtaposition of complementary colours produced discord and not harmony. The very rigid, doctrinaire approach of Seurat and Signac was bound to clash with his own desire to liberate painting from every kind of restriction.

In June 1886, he moved to Pont-Aven in Brittany, which was then a favourite resort of painters. He was attracted to it partly because it was a country with archaic customs and partly because living there was very cheap. 'I love Brittany, I find there the savage, the primitive. When my wooden shoes reverberate on this granite soil, I hear the muffled, heavy and powerful note I am seeking in painting.'

This urge to seek primitive, exotic terrain was carried a stage further in 1887 when he set out with the painter Charles Laval for Panama and Martinique. On Martinique the two artists lived in a negro hut, ate fishes and fruit, painted palm trees, banana trees and especially natives, and thought for a few blissful days that they had discovered Paradise. But Laval was taken ill with fever, while Gauguin himself suffered violent attacks of dysentery. Nevertheless, so far as work was concerned, this visit was not unprofitable. Gauguin made on Martinique a number of paintings which show him gradually freeing himself from Impressionism, simplifying his forms and, in the clear sunlight, using bolder colours including patches of blues, purple-mauves and reds (see Plate ix). 'Despite my physical weakness,' he said, 'I have never before made paintings so clear, so lucid.'

On his return from Martinique, Gauguin sought the hospitality of Schuffenecker (who had likewise given up his job at the bank to become a painter), then returned to Pont-Aven. In August he was joined there by Emile Bernard. Bernard had met Gauguin briefly during his first stay at Pont-Aven in 1886, but though arriving with an introduction from Schuffenecker, had not been well received — the two had in fact seen very little of each other. (At the pension Gloanec at Pont-Aven, Gauguin and his friends dined apart from the academic painters, and were referred to pugnaciously as 'The Impressionists'.) In 1888, however, Gauguin was very much interested in Bernard's recent paintings, executed in a style which Bernard and Anquetin had created under the influence of Japanese prints and Cézanne. This style was known as cloisonism because of its areas of unbroken colour surrounded by bold outlines; the forms being made to stand out in clear-cut silhouette. When Gauguin saw Bernard's *Breton Women in a Field* he was, so Bernard assures us, greatly impressed, and forthwith painted his own *Vision after the Sermon* (Plate xii) in which he used a similar convention reminiscent of Japanese prints and stained-glass.

The Vision after the Sermon depicts the moment after the sermon when the peasants, in their simplicity, almost imagine that they can see Jacob wrestling with the angel. The priest himself appears in the bottom right corner. Instead of a painting executed in front of nature, this is a work executed from memory and imagination — what Gauguin called an 'abstraction'. 'Real' figures — the peasants — are juxtaposed with imagined figures. The unreality of the scene is further enhanced by extremely arbitrary colour, in particular a background of flaming crimson. Instead of the typical Impressionist touch, there are flat or only slightly modelled areas of colour surrounded by bold strong outlines. The forms are simplified and in places given a distinct *art-nouveau* curvilinear character. A slight suggestion of recession is created by the overlapping of the forms and by the diminution in scale of the figures, but the general effect is rather like a polychrome bas-relief. The wrestling figures themselves were derived from a Japanese print, probably from one of the groups of wrestlers in Hokusai's *Mangwa*. When this picture was finished, Gauguin offered it to a church near Pont-Aven — not out of piety but because he wanted to see its effect in the setting of the Romanesque and Gothic forms of the granite chapel. But it was refused by the priest.

The Vision after the Sermon is a key work for the understanding of Gauguin's development — and indeed for the development of modern art — as it marks his clear break with Impressionism and the naturalistic movement. This was the period when the Symbolist literary movement was getting under way, when writers of the new generation were attacking naturalism for its subservience to nature and were exalting the creative power of the imagination. Though Emile Bernard was only twenty years old, he was a reader of Baudelaire and a friend of young writers like Albert Aurier. 'Attentive to the Symbolist literary movement,' he wrote, 'I wanted a parallel kind of painting.' Gauguin from this time on became likewise anti-naturalistic and spoke in the highest terms of the god-like creative capacity of the artist. For instance, in August 1888, probably just after painting *The Vision after the Sermon*, he wrote to Schuffenecker: 'A word of advice: don't paint too much direct from nature. Art is an abstraction! study nature, then brood on it and think more of the creation which will result, which is the only way to ascend towards God — to create like our Divine Master.' (There are echoes here of the ideas of Delacroix, Baudelaire and Edgar Allen Poe, all of whom Gauguin admired.) 'My latest works,' Gauguin went on, 'are on the right lines and I think you will find a new note, or rather the affirmation of my earlier experiments or synthesis of a single form and a single colour in which only the essential counts.'

From the time, in 1891, when Gauguin was acclaimed the originator of this new style, Bernard waged a bitter polemic to establish that he was the innovator and influenced Gauguin, that he was the true founder of the School of Pont-Aven. And up to a point, this was true. There does not seem to be much doubt that he did exert a very definite influence on Gauguin's style with paintings such as the *Breton Women;* on the other hand Gauguin was receptive to his cloisonism precisely because he had begun to develop along similar lines under the influence of Cézanne and Japanese prints. He carried the style to a new point of completeness and perfection and is beyond question that it was Gauguin and not Bernard who influenced painters such as Sérusier and the Nabis.

Gauguin and Bernard had both met Vincent van Gogh in Paris in 1886—7. Though van Gogh had gone to Arles in February 1888, and was working there in isolation, he was by no means out of touch with events at Pont-Aven. Bernard sent him many letters describing his new pictures, some of which he even illustrated with sketches. Vincent was at this time preoccupied with the idea of establishing a community of painters in his yellow house at Arles similar to the associations of Japanese artists: he specially wanted artists to exchange self-portraits as a token of sympathy and live together in a state of mutual help. In exchange for one of van Gogh's self-portraits, Gauguin sent him a self-portrait with a portrait of Bernard in the background (now in the collection of Vincent's nephew, V. W. van Gogh), while Bernard sent a similar picture.

On 8 October 1888, Gauguin wrote to Schuffenecker: 'This year I have sacrificed everything, execution and colouring, for style, intending to compel myself to do something different from what I usually do. It is a transformation which has not borne fruit so far, but will, I think, bear it.

'I have done a self-portrait for Vincent, who asked me for it. I believe it is one of my best things: absolutely incomprehensible (upon my word) so abstract it is. It looks at first like the head of a bandit, a Jean Valjean *(Les Misérables)*, but it also personifies a disreputable Impressionist painter burdened for ever with a chain for the world. The drawing is altogether peculiar, being complete abstraction. The eyes, the mouth, the nose, are like flowers in a Persian carpet, thus personifying also the symbolical side. The colour is a colour remote from nature; imagine something like pottery twisted by the furnace! All the reds and violets streaked like flames, like a furnace burning fiercely, the seat of the painter's mental struggles. The whole on a chrome background sprinkled with childish nosegays. Chamber of pure young girl. The Impressionist is such a one, not yet sullied by the filthy kiss of the Beaux-Arts (School).'

The painting is therefore done 'out of his head' not direct from nature; and the distortions are intended to convey symbolical ideas.

Ever since June van Gogh had been urging him to come to Arles, promising that his brother Theo, who was an art dealer with the firm of Goupil, would provide for him. Gauguin arrived at Arles later in that some month of October 1888.

The story of this tragic stay, which lasted two months, is well known. Gauguin and van Gogh lived in perpetual tension, arguing long into the night: the atmosphere was electric, dangerous. Though they used fairly similar conventions in art, their temperaments and tastes were strongly opposed. 'Vincent and I,' wrote Gauguin, 'are in general very little in agreement, above all with regard to painting. He admires Daumier, Daubigny, Ziem and the great Rousseau, whom I cannot stand. And on the other hand he detests Ingres, Raphael, Degas and all those whom I admire . . . He likes my paintings very much but when I have finished them, he always finds that I have made a mistake here, or there. He is romantic, while I am rather inclined towards a primitive state. When it comes to colour, he is interested in the accidents of the pigment, as with Monticelli, whereas I detest this messing about with the medium.'

These differences are very apparent if one compares, for instance, Gauguin's *Old Women of Arles* (Plate xiii) with a rather similar painting by van Gogh, *Promenade at Arles — Souvenir of the Garden at Etten*. Gauguin uses simple, almost geometrical forms; those of van Gogh are twisting, flame-like, emotionally very highly charged. And whereas Gauguin's brushwork is very restrained, van Gogh's is extremely personal and plays an important part in the effect. 'It is odd,' wrote Gauguin, 'that Vincent feels the influence of Daumier here: I, on the contrary, see the Puvis [de Chavannes] subjects in their Japanese colourings. Women here with their elegant coiffure have a Grecian beauty. Their shawls, falling in folds like the primitives, are, I say, like Greek friezes.' Though the exact dates of these two pictures are not known it seems probable that Gauguin's was done first and that van Gogh used it as his starting-point — for, unlike Gauguin, he needed to have something in front of him while he was painting, either nature or another work of art. The fact that Gauguin was trying to impose his method of working from memory upon him was one of the factors which led to the final crisis.

Gauguin and van Gogh painted each other's portrait. When Gauguin finished his picture of van Gogh painting sunflowers, van Gogh exclaimed: 'It is certainly me, but it's me gone mad.' 'That very evening,' wrote Gauguin, 'we went to the café. He took a light absinthe. Suddenly he flung the glass and its contents at my head. I avoided the blow and, taking him bodily in my arms, went out of the café, across the Place Victor Hugo . . .' On Christmas Eve, after trying to attack Gauguin with a razor, van Gogh cut off his own ear and sent it as a present to a girl in a brothel. Gauguin thereupon summoned Theo to Arles by telegram; then returned with him to Paris, without waiting to see Vincent again.

In Paris he stayed once more with the Schuffeneckers. His portrait of the Schuffenecker family (Plate xiv) executed at this time shows how his style was become suppler. There is more space, the figures are more directly treated, yet the simplification and strength of design have been retained. Schuffenecker — 'the good Schuff' — a timid, well-meaning little man, is said to have been dominated by the assertive personality of Gauguin who practically took over the house while he was there, removed Schuffenecker's pictures and hung his own in their place, appropriated his studio and, on at least one occasion, even locked the studio door in his host's face.

Gauguin paid a number of visits to the Paris World's Fair, which opened in the spring of 1889, and was particularly interested in the Javanese village and the Hindu dancers. Though not included in the official retrospective exhibitions of French art, Gauguin, Bernard, Schuffenecker, Laval, Monfreid, Fauché, Anquetin and Roy found an opportunity to show some of their paintings unofficially within the grounds of the exhibition, at the Café Volpini, under the title 'Groupe Impressionniste et Synthétiste'. However, nothing was sold.

About the end of May 1889, Gauguin returned to Pont-Aven. This third stay in Brittany, which lasted except for a break of four months until November 1890, was a period of great activity. Now more than ever Gauguin tried to capture the rustic, primitive character of the Breton scene, its melancholy and remoteness, in paintings of peasants working in the fields and in pictures inspired by their naive religious faith. *The Yellow Christ* (Plate xvi), for instance, was based on the wooden polychromed sculpture of Christ in the ancient chapel of Trémalo, near Pont-Aven, which he transposed to an open-air setting. Some of the artists in Brittany had found in him an outward resemblance to the figure of the Messiah, suggested by his grave, imposing manner, his wearing of a short beard and moustache, and his position as the leader of a group of disciples. In several paintings, notably in *Christ on the Mount of Olives*, Gauguin seized on this resemblance as a means of alluding simultaneously to his own loneliness and suffering. *The Breton Calvary* (Plate xvii) — painted after he had left Pont-Aven and moved to Le Pouldu on the coast — was inspired by one of the stone calvaries characteristic of the region, most probably the Romanesque calvary at Nizon. The colours were used for their emotional effect, to enhance the mood of brooding melancholy and poetry. On a visiting card found among the papers of Albert Aurier, he made some notes evidently related to this composition:

'Calvary cold stone from the soil — Breton idea of the sculptor who explains religion through his Breton soul with Breton costumes — Breton local colour . . . passive sheep' and on the reverse:

'All this in a Breton landscape i. e. Breton poetry his starting-point (colour brings the setting into a bluish harmony) etc. . . Cheerless to do In contrast — (the human figure) poverty [illegible word] of life —'

Unlike the Impressionists, who tried to eliminate the literary element from their paintings, Gauguin was now very interested in subject-matter and was even prepared at times to define it in words (though words that were deliberately poetic and imprecise).

Gauguin moved to Le Pouldu towards the end of September 1889, and on 2 October settled at the inn kept by Mlle Marie Henry. He was accompanied by Meyer de Haan, a Dutchman who had ceded an interest in a prosperous biscuit factory in Amsterdam in return for a monthly allowance, in order to devote himself to the fine arts. He had begun as an academic painter, but had soon developed an enthusiasm for Impressionism. He became a great admirer of Gauguin, to whom he had been recommended by Camille Pissarro, and helped him financially, even keeping him supplied with tobacco. Under Gauguin's direction his own talents matured rapidly: he produced several works, notably a self-portrait, which are of considerable interest.

At Le Pouldu, Gauguin was also joined by Sérusier and Filiger. Mlle Henry's inn became the centre of great artistic activity. The small living room was entirely transformed by Gauguin, de Haan and Sérusier. The window-panes were covered with

14

painted scenes of Brittany, like stained-glass windows. Wherever there was a space, mottoes and sayings were written on the plaster walls. Two landscapes and a portrait of Marie Henry by Meyer de Haan filled one wall; an over life-size bust of Meyer de Haan by Gauguin was placed on the mantelpiece; little statuettes and pots stood on shelves around the walls. A picture entitled *Bonjour, Monsieur Gauguins* (sic) was stuck on the upper panel of the door opening into the hall, and on the lower panel Gauguin painted *The Caribbean Woman* directly on the wood of the door. Outside the room, over the doorway, was a canvas entitled *The Terrestrial Paradise*.

A self-portrait and a portrait of Meyer de Haan were painted directly on the wooden doors of a massive cupboard, and the ceiling of the room was decorated with a painting of a swan and the head and shoulders of a woman (probably a reference to the Jupiter and Leda myth) surrounded by the inscription 'Honi soit qui mal y pense!' Gauguin referred sardonically in his self-portrait (Plate xviii) to the contrast between his outward resemblance to the Messiah and his arrogant and sensual inner nature, introducing as attributes not only a halo but the snake and apples symbolic of the Fall. In the companion picture, Meyer de Haan, who was bent and almost dwarf-like, was portrayed as the Devil. Thus the decorative scheme referred in part to the twin themes of Paradise and the Fall of Man.

It was at Le Pouldu in 1889 that Gauguin carved the bas-relief *Soyez amoureuses et vous serez heureuses* (page 20) — a clear reference to his own ideas on free love. 'Gauguin (as a monster) seizing the hand of a protesting woman and saying to her: Be in love and you will be happy. The fox, an Indian symbol of perversity, then some little figures in the interstices.' Stylistically, this relief is developed out of such pictures as *The Vision after the Sermon*, though it has a much more pronounced earthy and primitive character. The *art-nouveau* curves present in *The Vision after the Sermon* likewise play a larger part in the design. One only needs to compare it with an Impressionist landscape painted three years before to see how radically Gauguin's conception of art has changed. In *Soyez amoureuses et vous serez heureuses* there is an imagined event, a projection of the artist's fantasy, a symbol, conceived in a manner which is entirely arbitrary.

Towards the end of 1890, Gauguin returned to Paris where he came into touch with Symbolist writers like Jean Moréas, Charles Morice, Stéphane Mallarmé, Paul Verlaine and Octave Mirbeau and was welcomed by them as the leading representative of Symbolism in painting. He became an habitué of the cafés where the Symbolist writers foregathered; he attended several of Mallarmé's 'Tuesdays'; Octave Mirbeau wrote the preface to the catalogue of the sale of 30 of his pictures at the Hôtel Drouot;

and, shortly before his departure for Tahiti, a banquet was held in his honour at the Café Voltaire presided over by Mallarmé and attended by some thirty writers and artists of the Symbolist circle including Carrière, Redon, Morice, Moréas and Aurier.

Gauguin had been considering for some time the idea of going to the tropics, perhaps taking Emile Bernard, Laval or Meyer de Haan with him. His original intention had been to go once more to Martinique, or to Tonkin or Madagascar, but Pierre Loti's novel *Le Mariage de Loti* and an official description of the enchantments of the Pacific islands made him decide on Tahiti.

To the creative artists of the Third Republic, who found themselves in a society where they had no proper place, where money values alone seemed to count, the age-old dream of a lost Paradise and Golden Age was particularly compelling. Artists felt themselves stifled in a hostile environment from which they needed to escape. Some escaped by turning inwards, by cultivating the world of their imagination and by cutting themselves off from ordinary life. Mallarmé, Villiers de l'Isle-Adam, Odilon Redon, Gustave Moreau did this. Others escaped by physically leaving Europe and going away to some remote part of the globe where more primitive and congenial conditions prevailed. Loti did this. Rimbaud did first one and then the other.

Gauguin was attracted to Tahiti however not only as a means of escape and renewal (by a return to origins) but also because it provided new subjects for his paintings and because life there was said to be free from all money difficulties ' . . . one has only to raise an arm to find food'. In some respects he was to be cruelly disappointed. Tahiti was a French colony. On arriving at Papeete, the capital, he found that the Europeans were already established there. 'It was Europe, the Europe from which I had thought to free myself, and, into the bargain, all the irritating kinds of colonial snobbery.' After several months he moved some 25 miles from Papeete and took a native house and a native wife; he dressed himself like the natives, went on fishing expeditions with them and tried to familiarise himself with their customs and way of thought. Whereas Loti, who had also visited Tahiti and taken a native wife, remained always the civilised westerner, conscious of his own superiority, Gauguin felt he had much to learn from them.

The pictures executed during this visit to Tahiti show a further move towards a more direct treatment. Instead of the large areas of uniform colour bounded by firm outlines of his Breton period, we find a definite modelling achieved through a more traditional use of nuances, and less conspicuous outlines. In most cases, the foreground and middle distance are clearly established; there is no longer a bizarre cutting of figures by the edge of the canvas. The tendency is away from Japanese art, towards

16

Portrait of Mette, 1877. White Marble, height 13 in. (33 cm.). The Courtauld Institute of Art, London.

Manao Tupapau (The Spirit of the Dead Watches), c. 1893—95. Woodcut, coloured by hand and stencils, $8\frac{7}{16} \times 20\frac{1}{2}$ in. (22.7 × 52 cm.). The Art Institute of Chicago.

Te Po (Eternal Night), 1894—95. Woodcut, $8\frac{1}{8} \times 14$ in. (20.5 × 35.5 cm.). The Courtauld Institute of Art, London.

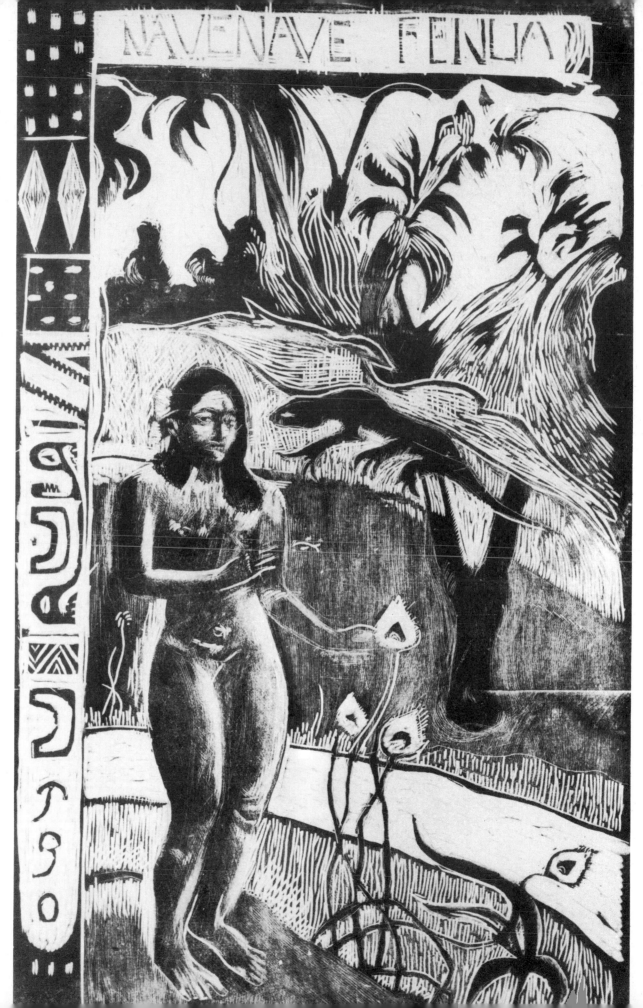

Nave Nave Fenua (The Delectable Earth), 1894—95. Woodcut, 13½×8 in. (34.5 × 20.3 cm.). The Courtauld Institute of Art, London.

Soyez amoureuses et vous serez heureuses (Be in love and you will be happy), 1889.
Wood relief, painted, $38\frac{1}{4} \times 28\frac{3}{4}$ in. (97.1 × 73 cm.). Museum of Fine Arts, Boston.

a more traditional treatment of space, modelling and composition. Certainly one never again finds paintings as stylised as *The Vision after the Sermon* or the *Self-Portrait with a Halo*.

A few of his Tahitian paintings — *Ia Orana Maria*, for instance — are of Christian themes, though the Biblical figures are enacted by Tahitians — Gauguin argued that the simple native folk would imagine them to be people like themselves. Another group of pictures is inspired by the traditional and pre-Christian religious beliefs and practices of the Polynesians. Gauguin stated in *Noa Noa* that his knowledge of the ancient pagan religions was mainly communicated to him by his wife. We know that this could not have been so. Not only were the religious secrets never revealed to women, but the traditional beliefs were more or less extinct by the time Gauguin reached Tahiti. His knowledge of them came from a book by an American consul to the South Sea Islands, named Moerenhout, published in 1837: *Voyages aux Iles du Grand Océan*. He transcribed passages from this book in his own manuscript *Ancien Culte Mahorie*, compiled about 1892, and used them again later almost word for word in the preparation of *Noa Noa*. His painting of *The Moon and the Earth* (Plate xxxii), for instance, was clearly inspired by the legendary Dialogue between Fatou and Hina (the spirits of the Earth and the Moon) regarding the eternity of Matter:

'Hina said to Fatou:

'— Revive man when he is dead.

'The God of the Earth replied to the Goddess of the Moon:

'— No, I shall not revive him.

'Man will die, vegetation will die, and all things that feed on it, the earth will die, the earth will finish not to be born again.

'Hina replied:

'— Do as you please. I for my part shall revive the *Moon*.

'And what was owned by Hina continued to exist, what was owned by Fatou perished, and man must die.'

When Gauguin portrayed the Tahitians worshipping their idols, he therefore depicted a practice which had ceased at least fifty or sixty years before. Similarly he looked back nostalgically to the days when Tahiti was ruled by Maori kings and queens (c. f. *Woman with Mangoes*, Plate xxxvi), and by the secret society of the Areois. Not content with Tahiti of his own day, he also sought the primitive, pre-European civilisation.

When Gauguin returned to Paris in September 1893, his first desire was to organise an exhibition of the works he had brought back with him from Tahiti. The exhibition opened at Durand-Ruel's two months later, with a catalogue preface by Charles Morice. Though it aroused considerable curiosity and was very much admired by his writer friends, only eleven pictures were sold; the public was bewildered not so much by the technical originality of Gauguin's style as by its own ignorance of the history, religion and customs of the Tahitians.

Fortunately Gauguin had a windfall: through the death of his uncle he received an inheritance of about 13,000 francs. This allowed him to rent an apartment in the rue Vercingétorix, an apartment which he decorated in characteristic fashion, just as he had previously decorated the living-room at Le Pouldu and his hut in Tahiti. (It seemed as though everything around him was turned into art.) He covered the windows of the tiny hall with paintings and embellished them with the characteristic motto 'Ici farùrù' (here people make love). He painted the walls of his large studio chrome yellow and hung them with paintings by himself, van Gogh and others, and with barbaric boomerangs, axes and spears. On Thursday evenings he gave informal receptions which were attended by Julien Leclercq, August Strindberg, Charles Morice, Paul Roinard, Aristide Maillol, Paul Sérusier and many other writers and artists.

His own person was equally remarkable, for he strode the streets of Paris wearing a long frock coat of blue, with buttons of mother-of-pearl. Beneath this was a blue waistcoat which buttoned down the side and sported a collar embroidered in yellow and green. He wore a hat of grey felt with a sky-blue ribbon; he carried, in place of a cane, a stick decorated by himself with barbaric carvings and inset with a splendid pearl. To complete his accoutrement, he took with him his mistress, a half-Indian, half-Malayan girl known as Annah the Javanese.

In April 1894 they went to Brittany, where Gauguin was joined once more by artists sympathetic to his ideas, including Armand Seguin and Roderic O'Conor. One day, as he and Annah were walking with Seguin at Concarneau, some boys began to throw stones at them and this ended in a brawl with four sailors of the locality. Gauguin was holding his own well enough until he caught his foot in a hole and in falling broke his ankle. Annah took advantage of his convalescence to return to Paris, where she ransacked his studio of everything except the pictures and then disappeared.

In September, Gauguin told Monfreid that he had resolved to sell all his works and go and live for ever in the South Seas. The sale, which took place at the Hôtel Drouot the following February, proved a disaster: he had to buy back the majority of the paintings and barely covered his expenses. Fortified, however, by a contract with

Lévy and Chaudet, who promised to ensure his financial security, he left for Tahiti in May 1895 — never to return.

His first visit to Tahiti had included much that was idyllic, the second was on the whole a time of misery: ill health and money difficulties plagued him almost without respite. His broken ankle had failed to heal completely and, in addition, he was suffering from the effects of syphilis contracted in Paris shortly before his departure. Within a few months, his legs were covered with open sores which caused intense irritation; indeed for long periods the pain was such that he was quite unable to work. With no money from Lévy and only small, irregular sums from Chaudet, he had to rely on what his faithful friend and correspondent Daniel de Monfreid could sell for him. Repeatedly in debt, he suffered spells of intense depression which reached their climax in January 1898 when he tried to commit suicide by taking arsenic. It was only after March 1900, when Vollard made a contract with him and arranged to send monthly remittances, that his financial position began to improve.

The atmosphere of tragedy is reflected in a certain number of his paintings executed in these years. It is very apparent, for instance, in the *Portrait of the Artist (at Golgotha)* (Plate xxxviii) painted in 1896 at a time when a succession of misfortunes led him to exclaim: 'I am so demoralised, discouraged, that I don't think it possible anything worse could happen.' The pale, worn face reveals his suffering and his weakened physical condition. It is clear also in the sombre, anguished colour harmonies of *D'Où Venons Nous? Qui Sommes Nous? Où Allons Nous?* (Plate xli) and *The White Horse* (Plate xlii), of 1897—98.

Gauguin has written of his Tahitian art in general:

'Wishing to suggest a luxuriant and wild nature, a tropical sun, which sets aflame everything around it, I have had to give my figures an appropriate setting. It is indeed life in the open air, but at the same time intimate; among the thickets, the shadowy streams, these whispering women in the immense palace decorated by Nature herself, with all the riches that Tahiti affords. Hence all these fabulous colours, this fiery yet softened and silent air.

' — But all that doesn't exist!

' — Yes, it exists, but as the equivalent of the grandeur, the profundity, of that mystery of Tahiti, when it has to be expressed on a canvas a metre square.

'She is very subtle, very clever in her naivety, the Tahitian Eve. The enigma hidden in the depths of her child-like eyes remains incommunicable... It is Eve after the fall, still able to walk naked without shame, preserving all her animal beauty as at the first day... Like Eve's, her body is still that of an animal. But her head has progressed with evolution, her mind has developed subtlety, love has imprinted an ironical smile upon her lips, and, naively, she searches in her memory for the *why* of present times. Enigmatically, she looks at you.'

Being himself a highly cultured western European, Gauguin was fascinated by the problem of Man's emergence from the primitive state, the life governed by instinct. Hence his recurrent references to Eve, to the Fall and to the Tree of Knowledge (themes which had begun to interest him even before his first visit to Tahiti). This can be seen for instance in his largest painting *D'Où Venons Nous? Qui Sommes Nous? Où Allons Nous?*, which Gauguin has described as follows — though warning 'Emotion first! understanding afterwards':

'In this big picture

    Where are we going?

Near the death of an old woman

A strange stupid bird concludes.

    What are we?

Day-to-day existence. The man of instinct wonders what all this means.

    Whence do we come?

Origins.

    Child.

        Common life.

'The bird concludes the poem by comparing the inferior being with the intelligent being in this great whole which is the problem indicated by the title.

'Behind a tree are two sinister figures, shrouded in garments of sombre colour, recording near the tree of knowledge their note of anguish caused by this knowledge itself, in comparison with the simple beings in a virgin nature, which might be the human idea of paradise, allowing everybody the happiness of living.'

Yet even with such a commentary as this, the precise significance of the painting remains obscure. As Gauguin himself said: 'My dream is intangible, it comprises no allegory.'

Gauguin contrasted his attitude to the literary content of his pictures with that of Puvis de Chavannes. 'Puvis explains his idea, yes, but he does not paint it. He is a Greek whereas I am a savage, a wolf in the woods without a collar. Puvis will call a picture *Purity* and to explain it will paint a young virgin with a lily in her hand — a hackneyed symbol, but which is understood by all. Gauguin, under the title *Purity*, will paint a landscape with limpid streams; no taint of civilised man, perhaps an individual.'

24

He rejected the academic symbolism of Puvis de Chavannes in favour of a more indirect, personal and evocative treatment. 'In painting, one must search rather for suggestion than for description, as is done in music.' Various contemporary poets were, of course, trying to do much the same — Verlaine, for instance, for whose *Romances sans Paroles* Gauguin had a particular admiration; and also Mallarmé. In the avoidance of the anecdote, the substitution of a situation that is equivocal and suggestive, demanding the imaginative co-operation of the observer, there is much in common between Gauguin's attitude to his subject-matter and that of the Symbolist poets. Odilon Redon, the only other painter of his generation developing along these lines, was also in close touch with the Symbolist writers.

At the same time, Gauguin referred repeatedly to the colours in his paintings in 'musical' terms — 'think of the highly important musical role which colour will henceforth play in modern painting' — and he insisted that colours should be used arbitrarily for their direct effect upon the emotions. When asked why he took liberties with colours, and for instance painted dogs red and skys rose, he replied:

'They are intended, absolutely! They are necessary and everything in my work is calculated, premeditated. It is music, if you like! I obtain by an arrangement of lines and colours, with the pretext of some sort of subject taken from life or from nature, symphonies, harmonies which represent nothing absolutely real in the vulgar sense of the word, which express directly no idea, but which provoke thoughts as music provokes thoughts, without the help of ideas or images, simply through the mysterious relationships which exist between our brains and these arrangements of lines and colours.'

These theories, which were an extension of ideas to be found in the writings of Delacroix and Baudelaire, again led on to modern art, even to abstract painting.

'The painter hasn't the task, like a mason, of building, compass in hand, a house to a plan furnished by an architect. It is good for the young to have a model, but let them draw a curtain over it while they paint it. It is better to paint from memory. Then what is yours will be yours; your sensation, your intelligence and your soul will get across to the beholder . . .

'Who tells you that it is necessary to seek colour contrasts? What is sweeter for an artist than to pick out in a bouquet of roses the hue of each? . . . Seek harmony and not contrast . . .

'Let everything suggest calm and peace of mind. Thus avoid movement in a pose. Each of your figures should be static.

'Study the silhouette of each object . . .

'Do not finish a work too much, an impression isn't sufficiently prolonged to allow one to search for infinite detail . . .'

In place of the instantaneous, snap-shot, view of the Impressionists, Gauguin avoids the momentary, the fleeting, the form in movement, and creates a world in which figures are charged with a slothful dignity. They look at us enigmatically, their eyes heavy with some secret thought.

In his reaction against Impressionism, Gauguin went for inspiration partly to Delacroix and Puvis de Chavannes (see, for example, Plates xl and xxxv). But he also — and this is part of his great historical importance as a pioneer of modern art — went to primitive and archaic sources. We have seen how he came to admire Romanesque sculpture and Japanese prints. While staying with Schuffenecker in Paris early in 1888, he started to make ceramics based on the primitive pottery in the Musée Guimet. Then, the following year, he introduced a Peruvian idol into his portrait *La Belle Angèle* (Plate xv). In 1889 he brought back with him from the Javanese pavilion at the World's Fair a fragment of a frieze representing a dancer, and was inspired by it to carve a statuette. When he went to Tahiti he took with him at least two photographs of the frieze of the Javanese Temple of Bârâbadour and at least one of an Egyptian wall painting. From this Javanese bas-relief he took not only the pose of individual figures as in *Ia Orana Maria*, but the frieze-like conception of *Faa Iheihe* (Plate xliii) of 1898 and related works. The inspiration of Egyptian wall paintings is obvious in *Ta Metete* (Plate xxix) of 1892. Fascinated by Polynesian art, he carved idol-like figures in a similar convention. Thus Gauguin sought inspiration in primitive and archaic art ('the great error is the Greek,' he said) in much the same way that the Mannerist artists of the sixteenth century turned to their Gothic forbears. In this respect he was of very great influence on the art of the twentieth century: for the discovery of the artistic merits of African wood-carving, so vital for the development of Cubism, was made by the Fauves and the German Expressionists under his direct influence.

Also important, though to a lesser degree, was his part in the revival of the woodcut, which in the middle of the nineteenth century had degenerated into a means for the mass-reproduction of pen drawings (such as those by Gustave Doré). Gauguin was one of the first to use large areas of black and to allow the tool marks to play their part in the design.

In 1901 he moved to the Marquesas Islands in order to live more cheaply and to find new subjects for his paintings. He had hoped to find a truly savage society there, but discovered instead that the European influences were once again causing a complete disruption of the traditional way of life. Within a few months of his arrival, he started to take the side of the natives against the white officials, defending their right not to send their children to the mission schools and protesting against the excessively heavy taxes and fines imposed upon them. A complaint about the corrupt behaviour of a policeman led to his being charged with libel and sentenced on 31 March 1903 to three month's imprisonment and a fine of 500 francs. At the time of his death on 8 May — a death which was almost certainly accelerated by the strain of these events — he was preparing to go to Tahiti to appeal against this sentence.

He had become a legend even in his lifetime. 'You are now,' so Monfreid wrote to him in December 1902, 'that unheard-of legendary artist, who from the furthest South Seas sends his disturbing, inimitable works, the definitive works of a great man who has as it were disappeared from the world.'

Recognition followed swiftly after his death. The memorial exhibition of his work at the Salon d'Automne of 1906, including no less than two hundred and twenty-seven paintings, drawings sculptures and prints from his abundant production, silenced his detractors and provided a triumphant vindication of his long years of struggle.

Outline Biography of Gauguin

1848

7 June   Paul Gauguin born in Paris, 52 rue Notre-Dame-de-Lorette, son of a journalist, Clovis Gauguin, and his wife Aline (née Chazel). One sister, Marie, born 1847.

1851

Clovis Gauguin set off with his family for Peru, where his wife had influential relations. He died on the voyage and was buried at Port Famine in the Straits of Magellan. His widow and the two children remained at Lima, Peru, until 1855.

1855

Mme Gauguin returned to France with the children. They lived until c. 1860 at Orleans in the family house owned by Isidore Gauguin, Paul's uncle, then apparently moved to Paris.

1865

December   At the age of seventeen and a half, Paul Gauguin entered the merchant service as novice on the *Luzitano*, on which he made two voyages between Le Havre and Rio de Janeiro.

1866

October 1866 —   December 1867. Second-lieutenant on the *Chili*, sailing between Le Havre and Valparaiso.

1867

7 July   Death of his mother Aline, who appointed Gustave Arosa as guardian of her two children.

1868

March 1868 —   April 1871. Served in the French navy aboard the cruiser *Jérôme Napoléon* (later renamed *Desaix*).

1871

On his return to Paris, found that his mother's house at St Cloud had been gutted by fire during the Franco-Prussian War.

28

Entered the office of the stockbroker Bertin, in Paris, rue Laffitte (a street in which there were also art galleries). Then, or a little later, met Emile Schuffenecker, who was also an employee at Bertin's. Began to paint.

1872

Encouraged by Schuffenecker and by Marguerite Arosa, his guardian's daughter, herself a painter, who taught him the technique of painting in oils.

1873
22 November   Married Mette Sophie Gad, a Danish girl aged 23.

1874
31 August   Birth of their first child, Emile.
Was becoming more and more interested in drawing and painting; went to the outskirts of Paris to paint on Sundays and sometimes visited the Atelier Colarossi with Schuffenecker in the evenings to draw from the model.

1875

About this time met Camille Pissarro and began to form a collection of Impressionist pictures.

1876

Was making a large income on the stock exchange. Had a landscape accepted at the Salon.

1877

Moved in the spring to a larger apartment at 79 rue des Fourneaux, rented from the sculptor Bouillot. Began to try his hand at modelling and carving under Bouillot's direction.
24 December   Birth of his daughter Aline.

1879
8 May   Birth of his second son Clovis.
Close friendship with Pissarro; apparently worked with him at Pontoise in the holidays. Was spending more and more time in the company of artists and dealers.

1880
1—30 April   Exhibited at the 5th Impressionist exhibition. Monet declined to exhibit, protesting that 'the little band has become a banal school which opens its doors to the first dauber that comes along'. Rented a house with a studio, 8 rue Carcel.

1881
2 April—1 May   Exhibited at the 6th Impressionist exhibition, when his *Study of a Nude* was highly

praised by Huysmans.

12 April	Birth of his third son, Jean. Spent the summer holidays with Pissarro and Cézanne at Pontoise. Towards the end of the year told Pissarro of his ambition to retire from business and devote himself full-time to painting.

1882

Played an active part in the organisation of the 7th Impressionist exhibition (in March). Huysmans commented: 'M. Gauguin is not progressing alas . . .'

In the course of the winter 1882—3 again visited Pissarro at Osny and painted with him.

1883

January	Resigned his job at the bank but apparently worked part-time until the end of the year.
15 June — 5 July	‚With Pissarro at Osny to spend the holidays and make some studies.
6 December	Birth of his fourth son, Paul (Pola).

1884

(?) January	Moved to Rouen, where he rented a house for a year. His resources were exhausted after three or four months and his attempts to sell his pictures were in vain.
early August	Mette left by sea for Denmark with Aline and the youngest of the boys, leaving him at Rouen with the other boys and the maid.
December	Gauguin arrived in Copenhagen. He had arranged to work as Scandinavian agent for Dillies et Cie, manufacturers of tarpaulins, and continued to work for them until about May 1885.

1885

Lived in an apartment at Gl. Kongevej 105, then moved on 22 April to Norregade 51.

1—6 May	Short one-man show at the Society of the Friends of Art, Copenhagen, was ignored by the press and a total failure.

(?) end June	Embittered by this lack of success and the hostility of his wife's family, he returned to Paris, taking Clovis with him.
September	Spent several days at Dieppe (where he met and quarrelled with Degas), then may have gone to London for two or three weeks.
October	Rented a small apartment, 10 rue Cail, Paris. Tried to get employment as assistant to Bouillot; also considered seeking a minor post on the stock exchange. Mette began to sell pictures from his collection. Spent the winter in miserable conditions.

1886

	With Clovis ill in bed, worked as a bill-poster to earn money to support them both. When Clovis had recovered, put him in a *pension* at Antony (Seine).
15 May — 15 June	Represented in the 8th and last Impressionist exhibition.
(?) June	Had a violent quarrel with Seurat over the use of Signac's studio.
late June — 13 November	Made his first visit to Pont-Aven, staying at the Pension Gloanec. The other boarders included Charles Laval and various English and American painters. First, but unproductive, meeting with Emile Bernard in August.
November — December	On his return to Paris in November, settled at 257 rue Lecourbe. Unable to sell any of his own works, living meagrely on the sale of pictures from his collection. Began to make ceramic sculpture in collaboration with the ceramist Chaplet. Saw much of Degas, but now avoided Pissarro and the Neo-impressionists. Met Vincent van Gogh. Spent most of December in hospital.

1887

	Apparently taught at the Académie Vitti.
Early April	Told Mette he was going to Panama 'to live as a *savage*'. She came to Paris to see him before his departure and to collect Clovis.
10 April	Left St Nazaire with Laval for Panama via Guadeloupe and Martinique, arriving in Panama at the end of April (with the intention of moving on to Taboga). Failed to get help from his brother-in-law Juan Uribe, who was in business there. Worked as

labourer on the canal to raise money to go to Martinique, while Laval worked as portrait painter.

June	On suspension of part of the work on the canal, both moved to Martinique, where they lived in a native hut. Laval stricken with fever.
July — August	Ill with dysentry contracted in Panama.
September	Began to paint again.
November	Worked his passage back to France on a sailing vessel (Laval remaining a few months longer). Went to stay with Schuffenecker, 29 rue Boulard; met Daniel de Monfreid there. Saw Vincent van Gogh again.

1888

January	Making ceramic sculpture with Chaplet. Exhibited with Pissarro and Guillaumin at Goupil's (the branch run by Theo van Gogh).
February — October	At Pont-Aven, Pension Gloanec. His health still troubling him and very pressed for money.
June	Received a letter from Vincent van Gogh inviting him to Arles. Joined at Pont-Aven by Laval, Moret, Chamaillard, Schuffenecker and (in August) by Emile Bernard. Painted *The Vision after the Sermon;* attracted by Bernard's sister, Madeleine.
September	Gave instruction to Sérusier, who painted the 'talisman' under his direction.
October	One-man show at Goupil's.
20 October	Joined Vincent van Gogh at Arles on the understanding that Theo would take part of his production in exchange for a monthly allowance.
December	Made a day trip to Montpellier with him to visit the museum.
24 December	Van Gogh cut off his own ear. Summoned Theo to Arles and returned with him to Paris after Christmas; went to stay with the Schuffeneckers.

1889

January — March	Paris, 25 Avenue Montsouris. Made a set of eleven lithographs on zinc.
February	Exhibited with Les XX at Brussels for the first time.
(?) March	Visited the World's Fair and was particularly interested in the Javanese and Indonesian art. Exhibited with Laval, Fauché, Schuffenecker, Anquetin, Monfreid, Bernard and Roy at the Café Volpini as 'Groupe Impressionniste et Synthétiste'.
end May or beginning June	Returned to Pont-Aven, Pension Gloanec, then moved shortly afterwards to Le Pouldu for about a month; back at Pont-Aven late June-late September. Accompanied by Meyer de Haan, and for part of the time by Sérusier, Laval, Chamaillard, Filiger, Moret and Jourdain. Helped financially by de Haan.
late September	Moved to Le Pouldu, staying first at the Auberge Destez-Portier.
2 October — (?) February	At the inn run by Mlle Marie Henry; decorated the living-room with the assistance of de Haan and Sérusier. Made unsuccessful attempts to get a post at Tonkin.
31 October — 11 November	Exhibition at the Society of the Friends of Art, Copenhagen, of French and Scandinavian Impressionists drawn mainly from the collection of Mette Gauguin and including works by Gauguin.

1890

(?) 8 February	Returned to Paris and called on Theo van Gogh to seek some kind of employment. Again stayed with the Schuffneckers, now living 14 rue Durand-Claye. Considered going to Madagascar or Tahiti.
June — 7 November	In Brittany with de Haan, moving between Pont-Aven and Le Pouldu; joined in July by Filiger and (briefly) by Sérusier. Squabbled with de Haan over the affections of Mlle Henry. Left her inn on 7 November owing more than 300 fr., abandoning his paintings there; returned to Paris.
November — December	In Paris, staying with the Schuffeneckers. Met Moréas, Morice, Carrière and other leading Symbolists and joined them at the Café Voltaire, the Côte d'Or, etc.

1891

1 January	His lithograph of Jean Moréas, inscribed 'Soyez Symboliste', published in *La Plume*.
	Introduced by Morice to Mallarmé; attended his 'Tuesdays' and etched his portrait.
3 February	Attended the banquet of the *Pèlerin Passionné* in honour of Moréas.
	Quarrelled with Schuffenecker and was asked to leave; moved to a hotel, rue Delambre; invited by Monfreid to paint in his studio, 55 rue du Château. Exhibited with Les XX at Brussels. Great activity to advertise his sale; articles by Mirbeau and Aurier.
23 February	His sale of 30 paintings at the Hôtel Drouot realised about 9350 frs., but led to a break with Emile Bernard.
7 March	Arrived in Copenhagen to see his wife and children for what proved to be the last time (back in Paris by 20 March, perhaps by 15th).
23 March	Banquet in his honour at the Café Voltaire presided over by Mallarmé.
26 March	The Ministry of Public Instruction and Fine Arts granted him, at his request, an 'unpaid artistic mission' in Tahiti, which enabled him to get a passage at a reduced rate.
4 April	Left Paris for Tahiti. Travelled via Melbourne, Sydney and Noumea.
21 May	Performance at the Théâtre d'Art for the benefit of Verlaine and Gauguin showed a loss.
23 May	Joyant, Theo's successor at Goupil's, gave 835 fr. to Morice, which he failed to forward.
8 June	Arrived in Tahiti. Took a hut in Papeete and tried to learn the Maori language; death of Pomare V, the last king of Tahiti, shortly after his arrival; studies of landscapes and portraits. Titi, a somewhat Europeanised Tahitian, was his *vahine*.
(?) October	Went to live in the district of Mataiea, some 25 miles from Papeete, surrounded only by natives.
(?) December	Took Tehura as his *vahine*.

34

1892

February   Seriously ill and in hospital, spitting blood. May have begun at this time to read Moerenhout's book an Tahitian lore and compile his own *Ancien Culte Mahorie*.

March   'My life is now that of a savage . . . I am working more and more.' Living mainly on roots and fish.

June   Thought of leaving though wished to stay. Had received no money from France and was very hard up; sold a painting for 400 fr. at Papeete to the captain of a schooner.

12 June   Wrote to the Director of Fine Arts in Paris, asking to be repatriated; owing to administrative difficulties this was not effected until the following year.

August   Sold two small wood sculptures in Papeete for 300 fr.

September   One of his Tahitian pictures *(Woman with a Flower)* exhibited at Goupil's.

November   Received 300 fr. from Monfreid.

December   The dealer Portier returned his unsold Gauguins to Monfreid as none of his clients was interested.

1893

Feb – April   Subsisting on breadfruit and water; his eyesight impaired, did very little painting for two months.

24 March   Joyant returned all Gauguin's paintings, ceramics, etc., that were on consignment at Goupil's.

26 March   Exhibition of some 50 of his paintings, sculptures and ceramics opened in Copenhagen (in the building of Free Exhibition); was simultaneously represented in another exhibition there at the Kleis Gallery. These exhibitions aroused great interest and some works were sold.

April   Received 700 fr. from Mette and paid his debts.

May   Repatriated to France via Noumea and Sydney.

30 August	Arrived at Marseilles with 4 fr. in his pocket; received money from Sérusier. In Paris, rented a studio 8 rue de la Grande Chaumière.
September	Called to Orleans in connection with an inheritance of about 13,000 fr. from his uncle Isidore Gauguin.
November	Exhibition of his Tahitian works (44 paintings and 2 sculptures) at the Galerie Durand-Ruel; eleven paintings sold. The catalogue preface was by Charles Morice, with whom he began to write *Noa Noa*.
December	Rented a studio, 6 rue Vercingétorix. Gave receptions on Thursdays attended by, among others, Leclercq, Morice, Roinard, Mollard, Maillol, Seguin, O'Conor, Zuloaga, Monfreid, Chamaillard, Maufra and Strindberg.

1894

February	Exhibited with La Libre Esthétique at Brussels. Made a brief trip to Brussels, Antwerp and Bruges with Julien Leclercq; attended the opening of La Libre Esthétique and admired the Memlings at Bruges. Annah the Javanese joined him as his mistress.
April	Stayed at Le Pouldu with Annah for several weeks as guests of the Polish painter Slevinsky, then moved to Pont-Aven, where he settled at the Pension Gloanec; accompanied at various times by Chaudet, Seguin, Chamaillard, Moret, Loiseau and O'Conor.
25 May	While walking with Annah and Seguin at Concarneau was involved in a brawl with sailors and had a foot broken. This caused intense pain and for three months he was apparently unable to paint. During his convalescence, made woodcuts from memory of some of his Tahitian pictures.
(?) September	Annah returned to Paris, where she ransacked his studio of everything except the pictures and then disappeared.
20 September	Wrote to Monfreid that he had resolved to go and live for ever in the South Seas; hoped to leave with Seguin and O'Conor.

36

14 November	His action against Mlle Henry for the recovery of his pictures left at Le Pouldu in 1890 was dismissed by the court at Quimperlé.
(?) late November	Returned to Paris, rue Vercingétorix. Worked part of the time in O'Conor's studio, 102 rue du Cherche Midi.

1895

January	Contracted syphilis.
17 January	Attended the banquet in honour of Puvis de Chavannes.
18 February	His sale (largely of Tahitian works) at the Hôtel Drouot was a disaster; he had to buy back most of the paintings.
(?) May	Sailed to Tahiti, via Auckland, New Zealand.
July	Arrived in Tahiti to find Papeete increasingly Europeanised. At first intended to move the next month to the Marquesas Islands, but instead built a large hut in the country at Punavia.
November	In despair because no one had paid the money due to him.

1896

April — May	His broken ankle causing much pain; had also developed sores on his legs. Wrote in May that he was in desperate need of money, at the end of his strength and resources.
June	Asked Monfreid (and likewise Maufra) to find fifteen people interested in his paintings who would contribute 160 fr. a year each in return for a painting apiece.
July	In hospital but with no money to pay the bill. Left hospital a month later only partly cured and owing 140 fr. Schuffenecker circulated a petition (signed by Puvis de Chavannes, among others) asking the State to aid him; was sharply reproved by Gauguin.
October	Received 400 fr. and paid some of his debts. 'I am so demoralised, discouraged, that I don't think it possible anything worse could happen.'

November	Feeling somewhat better.
December	Had received a little money, but was still 900 fr. in debt.

1897

January	Received 1,200 fr. from Chaudet with the promise of a further 1,600 fr., and was out of debt. Apparently re-entered hospital in the hope of being completely cured.
February	Feeling much better, was hard at work.
24 February — 1 March	Exhibited with La Libre Esthétique at Brussels.
April	Received a letter from his wife announcing the death of Aline, his favourite child. Through his landlord's death, was obliged to move to another site and reconstruct his house; had not received the 1,600 fr. promised by Chaudet.
May	Borrowed 1,000 fr. from the bank for a year to buy land and construct a new house.
July	Had exhausted his money and was becoming very worried about his debts. Ill with sores on his legs and suffering from double conjunctivitis, was unable to paint for some four months.
August	Wrote a harsh letter to Mette, who broke off the correspondence.
September	Now owed 1,800 fr. and had no more credit.
November	Was vomiting blood; told Monfreid he wanted only silence, to be left in peace and forgotten.
December	In despair because of growing debts, ill-health and the difficulty of selling his works, began to paint *D'Où Venons Nous?* as a last great painting. Living on water, guavas and mangoes.

1898

January	Tried to commit suicide by taking arsenic.

38

February	Still ill from the effects of the poison. Received 700 fr. from Chaudet and 150 fr. from Maufra and paid his most pressing creditors.
March	Calmer and feeling better. Though no longer pursued by creditors, was worried by the debt due to the bank in May.
April	Having no money at all, took a clerical post in the Office of Public Works at Pepeete. Said that he had ceased to paint until things became normal again.
May	Received 575 fr. from Monfreid; also obtained an extension of credit on the 1,200 fr. now owing to the bank.
August	Received 700 fr. from Chaudet and was out of debt.
September	In hospital to have his foot treated.
October	Received 1,300 fr. from Monfreid and Chaudet. Vollard bought four pictures from Monfreid for 600 fr.
December — January	Exhibition of his recent paintings at the Galerie Vollard, including *D'Où Venons Nous?*
December	Vollard bought nine more paintings from Monfreid for 1,000 fr.

1899

January — February	Received money from Monfreid and was able to return to Punavia. Found that rats had destroyed the roof of his hut and that some drawings and an unfinished canvas had been destroyed by cockroaches. Still too ill to paint. Greatly upset that Vollard had obtained a number of his recent works at such low prices.
May	Spent money on constructing a well and had only 100 fr. in hand.
June	Had to obtain his bread on credit. Began to contribute articles to *Les Guêpes* (a monthly periodical published at Papeete), attacking the colonial administration and in particular the procurator.

August	Had no more canvas and was still too discouraged to paint. Published the first issue of his own satirical periodical *Le Sourire;* continued to issue this monthly until April 1900.
September	Started to work again, taking up a number of things left unfinished.
December	Suffering from the sores on his feet and in debt.

1900

January	Learnt of the death of Chaudet, who owed him about 2,000 fr. Received a letter from Vollard offering to buy watercolours, flower pictures, perhaps his entire output. Asked in reply for a monthly allowance of 300 fr. against pictures to be credited at 200 fr. each. Also received a letter from Prince Bibesco containing 150 fr. for a small painting. Was in great need of money.
March	Vollard accepted his terms and sent a first remittance.
May	Received 750 fr. from Monfreid and 300 from Vollard; paid his debts and had a little in hand. Also received an offer from Bibesco to take works in place of Vollard on the same terms. Said he had been unable to paint for six months.
August	Ill with influenza.
November	Because Vollard was in arrears with his monthly remittances, had to work as an accountant to pay for a new roof on his hut and to buy food.
December	Received 1,200 fr. from the collector Gustave Fayet in payment for two pictures. Entered hospital.

1901

Jan—Feb	In hospital, very ill with eczema on his feet and influenza.
April	Again unwell with influenza. The monthly remittances from Vollard now enabled him to live in comparative comfort, though the cost of living in Tahiti was rising sharply. In order to live more cheaply and to find new subjects for his paintings, decided to move to the Marquesas Islands.
(?) June	Sold his property for 4,500 fr.

August	Embarked for the Marquesas Islands.
16 September	Arrived at Atuana, the chief village of Hiva-Oa (La Dominique).
27 September	Bought a demi-hectare of land there from the mission. His house, known as the 'Maison du Jour', was completed by the end of October; it was in the centre of the village but surrounded by gigantic tropical plants.

1902

March	Work progressing well, though his health still poor. Refused to pay a tax which he judged excessive.
April	Defended the right of the natives not to send their children to the mission schools.
August	Now out of debt and had even saved a little; the cost of living much lower than on Tahiti. Was beginning to spend considerable sums on food, wine, absinthe, etc.
25 August	Wrote to Monfreid that he contemplated returning to France to be cured and then going on to paint in Spain for several years.
September	Sent the manuscript of *Racontars de Rapin* to André Fontainas in the hope that it would be published in the *Mercure de France*.
October	Received 600 fr. from Monfreid. Had received nothing from Vollard since April.
November	Complained to the Governor of the French Possessions in the South Seas about the high taxation of little direct profit to the islands, and the excessively heavy fines imposed on the natives.
1902 — 1903	Wrote *Avant et Après*.

1903

January	His house slightly damaged by a cyclone.
February	Wrote to the administrator of the Marquesas Islands to denounce the corrupt behaviour of a gendarme on a neighbouring island; this led to his being charged with libel. Also complained to the visiting inspectors about the unfair methods of administering justice to the natives. Because of the suffering caused by his eczema, he had been

unable to paint for nearly three months; his eyesight was also giving him cause for serious disquiet.

31 March   Was found guilty of libel and sentenced to three months in prison and a fine of 500 fr.

April   Planned to go to Tahiti to appeal against the sentence; anxious to raise money to meet the expenses. Told Monfreid: 'All these preoccupations are *killing me*.'

8 May   Died at Atuana.

Notes on the Plates

(All the paintings reproduced are oil on canvas unless otherwise stated)

Plate i. *Landscape*, 1873. 19⅞×32⅛ in. (50.5×81.5 cm.). The Fitzwilliam Museum, Cambridge. One of Gauguin's earliest surviving pictures. It is inscribed '7:73' and was presumably painted in July 1873, about four months before his marriage to Mette. The scene is perhaps on the outskirts of Paris or in Normandy. It shows the influence of early Corot and the Barbizon painters. Clearly painted on the spot, out of doors.

Plate ii. *The Seine at the Pont d'Iéna*, 1875. 25¼×36¼ in. (64×92 cm.). Musée du Louvre, Paris. The Pont d'Iéna in Paris. In this case the relationship seems closest to Jongkind; there is still no definite trace of Impressionism. A very accomplished rendering of wintry light and open space.

Plate iii. *Study of a Nude* (The Seamstress), 1880. 45×31¼ in. (114.5×79.5 cm.). Carlsberg Glyptotek, Copenhagen. The model for this picture was Justine, the maid who looked after Gauguin's children; she had posed in her youth for Delacroix. Gauguin painted her in her own room, in the act of doing her mending, an attitude so natural and unselfconscious that it makes even the nudes of Courbert look rhetorical. There is a marked interest in the fall of light, but the colours are rather drab.

When exhibited at the Impressionist exhibition in 1881, this picture was highly praised by Huysmans for its realism. It was afterwards purchased from Mette in 1892 by the Danish painter Philipsen.

Plate iv. *Winter Scene*, 1883. 23⅝×19⅝ in. (60×50 cm.). Carlsberg Glyptotek, Copenhagen. The artist's garden, 8 rue Carcel, Paris. A larger version of the same scene, dated 1883 and with two figures added in the foreground, is in the collection of S. Kiaer, Copenhagen. It is a delicate essay in Impressionism, reminiscent of the snow landscapes of Camille Pissarro.

Plate v. *Self-Portrait in front of an Easel*, 1884–85. 25⅝×21⅜ in. (65×54.5 cm.). Dr. Jacques Körfer, Berne. Painted during Gauguin's stay in Copenhagen. While Mette was using the drawing-room to give French lessons to young members of the nobility, Gauguin had to take refuge in a small attic bedroom which was lit by a narrow fanlight. He had only himself for model and stayed there alone during the long months of winter, painting his own portrait. This picture, obviously painted looking into a mirror, is a direct and objective study of his appearance; it is the work of a powerful temperament, the expression of his firm resolve to succeed as a painter.

Plate vi. *Still Life with Mandoline*, 1885. 24×20 in. (61×51 cm.). Musée du Louvre, Paris. A carefully formalised arrangement which shows the influence of Cézanne, particularly in the simplification of the shapes and the firm, precise outlines. Part of one of Gauguin's landscapes appears on the wall behind. Gauguin was very fond of playing the mandoline and the guitar.

Plate vii. *The Coast at Dieppe*, 1885. 28⅛×28⅛ in. (71.5×71.5 cm.). Carlsberg Glyptotek, Copenhagen. Painted during his brief visit to Dieppe in the autumn of 1885.

Plate viii. *Still Life with Decanter and Cherries*, 1886. Oil on panel, 21¾×23 in. (55×58.5 cm.). The Hon. Michael Astor, London. The inscription shows that this was painted in the Pension Gloanec during his first visit to Pont-Aven. Though Impressionist in its study of light, shadows and reflections, it also reveals the influence of Cézanne, notably in the inclined perspective of the table top and the introduction of flowered wallpaper as a background.

Plate ix. *Martinique Landscape*, 1887. 44½×33½ in. (113×85 cm.). The National Gallery of Scotland, Edinburgh. The pictures executed on Martinique marked a move away from Impressionism towards a form of decoration. In this splendid landscape, Gauguin has used flat patches of colour to create a rich decorative pattern, like a tapestry.

Plate x. *Breton Bathers*, 1888. 36½×28½ in. (91.5×72.5 cm.). Biggins Gallery, London. Gauguin executed a group of paintings of bathers at Pont-Aven in June—

July 1888. 'They are not at all like Degas . . . completely Japanese, by a savage of Peru.'

Plate xi. *Brittany Landscape*, 1888. 36¼×28¼ in. (92×72 cm.). Mr & Mrs Niarchos Collection, Paris. Painted at Pont-Aven. Though he has not yet broken completely with the Impressionist vision, Gauguin is trying here to create a pattern by means of simplified areas of contrasting colours, somewhat after the manner of Japanese prints.

Plate xii. *The Vision after the Sermon*, 1888. 28¾×36¼ in. (73×92 cm.). The National Gallery of Scotland, Edinburgh. Also known as *Jacob wrestling with the Angel*. This picture, painted after seeing Bernard's *Breton Women in a Field*, is discussed at length on pages 10-11. It is the masterpiece of his Synthetist phase.

Plate xiii. *Old Women of Arles*, 1888. 28¾×36 in, (73×91.5 cm.). Mr & Mrs L. L. Coburn Collection, The Art Institute of Chicago. Painted while he was staying at Arles with van Gogh (see p. 12). One of Gauguin's most stylised compositions, very much influenced by Japanese prints. A path with a bench appears in the top left and a pond with goldfish on the right. The background is seen in steep perspective; flat planes of colour create a strong decorative pattern. All the figures have been placed to one side of the picture.

Plate xiv. *The Schuffenecker Family*, 1889. 28¾×36¼ in. (73×92 cm.). Musée du Louvre, Paris. Painted early in 1889, while he was staying with the Schuffeneckers after his return from Arles. Theo van Gogh wrote to Vincent on 19 January 1889: 'He is still temporarily at the Schuffeneckers and is going to do the portrait of the whole family.' Gauguin's friend and biographer Rotonchamp refers to a version inscribed 'Je vote pour Boulanggg . . . [Boulanger].' The pictures on the wall are a still life by Gauguin and a Japanese print from his collection.

Plate xv. *La Belle Angèle*, 1889. 36¼×28½ in. (92×72 cm.). Musée du Louvre, Paris. A portrait of Angèle Satre painted at Pont-Aven. M. and Mme Satre, who lived next door to the Pension Gloanec, were friends of Gauguin who painted this picture for them as a present. He considered it his most successful portrait to date, but the sitter herself took fright at its rough vigour and stylisation and declined to accept it. It was afterwards included in his auction in 1891, when it was bought by Degas for 450 francs.

The picture is divided asymetrically into two parts, each with its own space. The object on the left is a Peruvian idol.

Plate xvi. *The Yellow Christ*, 1889. 36¼×29 in. (92×73.5 cm.). The Albright Art Gallery, Buffalo (Charles Clifton, James G. Forsyth, Elisabeth H. Gates, Charles W. Goodyear, Edmund Hayes and Sherman S. Jewett Funds). Begun at Pont-Aven and finished after Gauguin's final move to Le Pouldu. The figure of Christ was based on a wooden, polychromed crucifix in the chapel of Trémalo, near Pont-Aven. The village of Pont-Aven and the Colline Sainte-Marguerite appear in the background.

A little later, probably in 1890, Gauguin painted a self-portrait with the upper part of *The Yellow Christ* on the wall behind his head (the pose in reverse, seen looking into a mirror).

Plate xvii. *The Breton Calvary*, 1889. 36¼×29 in. (92×73.5 cm.). Musées Royaux des Beaux-Arts, Brussels. Also known as 'The Green Christ'. Painted at Le Pouldu; probably inspired by the Romanesque calvary at Nizon.

Plate xviii. *Self-Portrait with a Halo*, 1889. Oil on panel, 31¼×20¼ in. (79.5×51.5 cm.). National Gallery of Art, Washington. D. C. (Chester Dale Collection). Painted directly on the right-hand door of a massive cupboard at Le Pouldu (see p. 15). A companion picture of Meyer de Haan as the Devil was painted on the left-hand door.

Plate xix. *Still Life*, 1889. 19⅜×21½ in. (49×54.5 cm.). Sir Robert Adeane, London. In the autumn of 1889 Gauguin met the Countess de Nimal and her daughter in Brittany and succeeded in interesting them in his work. Having great hopes that the Countess would use her influence on his behalf, he dedicated this still life to her, and included a dog — possibly her own pet — in the upper corner.

A strong influence of Japanese prints. Some flattening of the picture space, a bizarre cutting of the forms by the edges of the picture, a decentralised composition.

Plate xx. *Bonjour Monsieur Gauguin*, 1889. 36½×29 in. (113×92 cm.). The National Gallery, Prague. This is not the painting which was stuck on the upper panel of the door opening into the hall at Le Pouldu (see p. 15) but an enlarged and improved version. The original painting is reproduced in *L'Oeil*, July—August 1959, p. 38.

II

VIII

X

P. Gauguin 88

XII

XIII

XIV

XVIII

XIX

XX

XXI

XXIII

XXV

XXVI

XXVII

XXVIII

TA MATETE

P Gauguin 92

XXIX

XXX

Gauguin 93.   Tefatou.

XXXII

XXXIV

NAVE NAVE MAHANA
P. Gauguin 1896

XXXV

XXXVI

XXXVII

XXXVIII

XXXIX

XL

XLI

XLII

XLIV

XLV

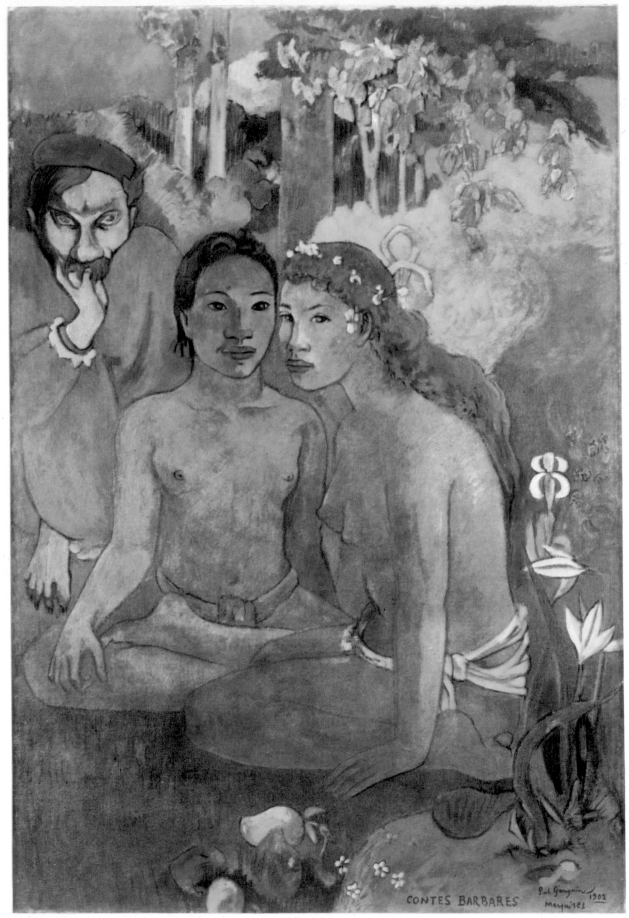

CONTES BARBARES   Paul Gauguin 1902
                        Marquises

XLVI

XLVII

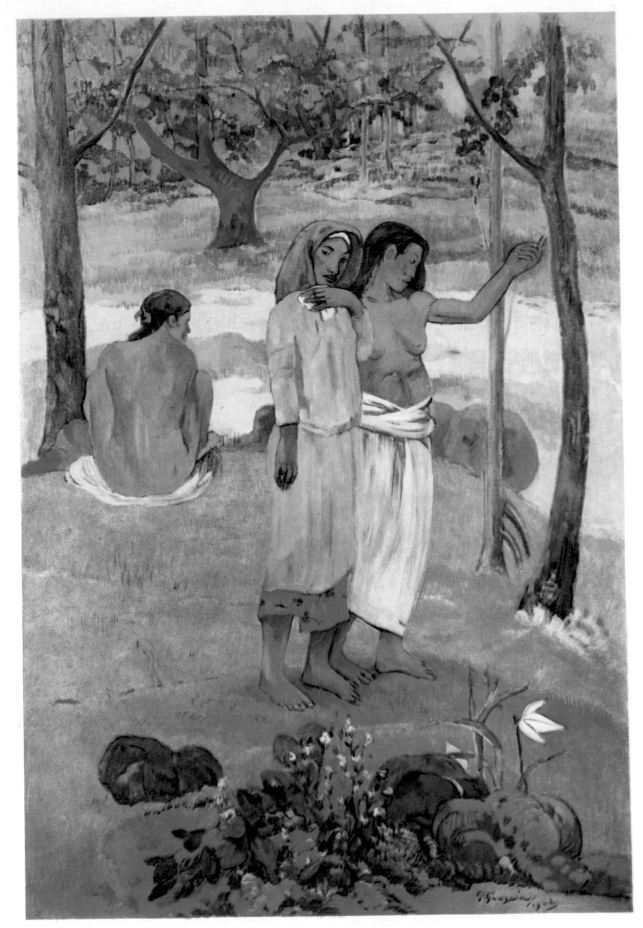

XLVIII

The title was inspired, somewhat ironically, by Courbet's *Bonjour Monsieur Courbet*, which Gauguin had seen in the museum at Montpellier in December 1888. With grim humour, Gauguin has made himself appear seedy, lonely and miserable — a rather alarming apparition. There is an effect of light breaking through storm clouds.

Plate xxi. *Landscape: Le Pouldu,* 1890. 29 × 36½ in. (73.5 × 92.5 cm.). Maresco Pearce, Esq., London. Gauguin and Bernard both painted a number of Breton harvest scenes in 1889 and 1890.

Plate xxii. *Marie Derrien,* 1890. 25⅝ × 21½ in. (65 × 54.5 cm.). The Joseph Winterbotham Collection, The Art Institute of Chicago. Formerly regarded as a portrait of Marie Henry, though it is not very much like her; the sitter actually seems to have been Marie Derrien, whose nickname was Marie 'Lagadu', meaning in Breton dialect, 'Black Eyes'. The painting in the background (considerably exaggerated in size) is the still life by Cézanne from Gauguin's collection. The treatment of the figure recalls some of Cézanne's portraits of Mme Cézanne in its simplification, firm modelling and rhythmical design.

Plate xxiii. *The Loss of Virginity,* 1890 – 91. 35 × 52 in. (89 × 132 cm.). Walter P. Chrysler, Jr. Collection, New York. Rotonchamp records that this picture was painted in Paris in the winter of 1890 – 91 as a result of Gauguin's close association with the Symbolist writers. 'In the execution of this picture Gauguin was much less concerned with pictorial considerations than with putting into practice certain literary theories which are incompatible with painting.' A virgin is seized by the demon of physical desire, as represented by a fox, an Indian symbol of lasciviousness. In the distance, a Breton wedding procession makes its way along a narrow path. Bold, saturated colours, but a lack of unity between figure and setting.

The landscape background was abstracted from *Landscape: Le Pouldu* (Plate xxi). As model for the girl, Gauguin used his mistress, Juliette Huet, who bore him a daughter some months after his departure for Tahiti.

Plate xxiv. *Vahine No Te Tiare* (Woman with a Flower), 1891. 27¾ × 18¼ in. (70.5 × 46.5 cm.). Carlsberg Glyptotek, Copenhagen. Painted within a few months of his arrival in Tahiti. It was the first of his Tahitian pictures to be seen in France.

Plate xxv. *Women of Tahiti,* 1891. 27 × 35½ in. (69 × 90 cm.). Musée du Louvre, Paris. Two Tahitian women squatting on a beach; the sea in the background. A more or less straightforward representation of the appearance of his models, without any poetic or mystical overtones. Though the figures are given their full weight and volume, the tipped perspective of the beach and the areas of contrasting colours create a decorative pattern.

A later variant of this composition, inscribed 'Parau Api' (The Day's News) and dated 1892, is in the Gemäldegalerie, Dresden.

Plate xxvi. *Tahitian Flowers,* c. 1891. 37½ × 24¼ in. (90.5 × 61.5 cm.). Mr & Mrs Niarchos Collection, Paris. One of Gauguin's most ambitious and sumptuous still lifes. It has been dated as late as 1901, but because of its rather precise rendering of detail and its strong colour contrasts is more likely to have been painted during his first visit to Tahiti. The mask in the background adds a note of mystery.

Plate xxvii. *Tahitian Landscape,* c. 1891. 26¾ × 36¾ in. (68 × 92.5 cm.). The Minneapolis Institute of Arts, The Julius C. Eliel Memorial Fund. Writing in *Noa Noa* of his first attempts at painting in Tahiti, Gauguin declared: 'The landscape, with its bold, intense colours, dazzled and blinded me.' This picture, closer to nature than *I Raro Te Oviri,* was probably painted towards the end of 1891.

Plate xxviii. *I Raro Te Oviri* (Under the Pandanus Trees), 1891. 29 × 36 in. (74 × 91.5 cm.). The Minneapolis Institute of Arts, The William H. Dunwoody Fund. The figures are based on sketches in Gauguin's Tahitian sketchbook; the composition is more stylised and imaginative than *Women of Tahiti* (Plate xxv). Brilliant, unreal colours convey an impression of the blazing tropical light, while the sinuous lines in the foreground are used both structurally and to create a rhythmical pattern.

Another version of *I Raro Te Oviri,* also dated 1891, is in the collection of Dr and Mrs David M. Levy, New York.

Plate xxix. *Ta Matete* (The Market), 1892. 29½ × 36¼ in. (75 × 92 cm.). Kunstmuseum, Basel. L.-J. Bouge has translated the title as 'We shall not go to market today' (because they are wearing their best dresses).

The attitudes of the seated figures, heads and feet in profile, with stiff, conventionalised gestures, were derived from Egyptian art. The forms are arranged in a series of planes parallel to the picture surface, like the wings on a stage.

Plate xxx. *Parau Parau* (Conversation), 1892. 30 × 37¾ in. (76 × 96 cm.). Mr & Mrs John Hay Whitney Collection, New York. A scene of everyday life in Tahiti. The attitude of the girl on the left was derived from Javanese sculpture, the circle of seated women from *Les Parau Parau* (Pushkin Museum, Moscow), a painting made by Gauguin the previous year.

Plate xxxi. *Nafea Foa Ipoipo* (When shall we be married?), 1892. 41¼ × 30½ in. (105 × 77.5 cm.). Kunstmuseum, Basel. Gauguin wrote to Mette in July 1892: 'I am hard at work, now that I know the soil and its odour, and the Tahitians whom I represent in a very enigmatic manner are none the less Maoris and not Orientals of the Batignolles (a part of Paris). It has taken me almost a year to understand this.'

Plate xxxii. *Hina Te Fatou* (The Moon and the Earth), 1893. 45 + 24½ in. (112.5 × 61 cm.). The Museum of Modern Art, New York, Lillie P. Bliss Collection. This depicts the legendary dialogue between Hina, the spirit of the Moon, and Fatou, the spirit of the Earth.

Plate xxxiii. *Mahana No Atua* (The Day of the God), 1894. 26 × 34¼ in. (66 × 108 cm.). The Art Institute of Chicago, Helen Birch Bartlett Memorial Collection. During his stay in France between the two visits to Tahiti, Gauguin made several pictures of Tahitian subjects, as well as a series of woodcuts. He had already made up his mind to return to Tahiti and his thoughts were preoccupied with the writing of *Noa Noa*. This picture embodies his idealised conception of life in Tahiti before the arrival of the Europeans.

The idol of the god Taaroa (creator of the Universe) was inspired partly by Indian art; the trees in the upper left were apparently derived from the pandanus trees in *I Raro Te Oviri* (Plate xxviii).

Plate xxxiv. *Breton Landscape: The Mill*, 1894. 28¾ × 36¼ in. (73 × 92 cm.). Musée du Louvre, Paris. The Moulin David at Pont-Aven, with the Colline Sainte-Marguerite in the background. Gauguin painted only a small number of pictures of Brittany in 1894 and they differ from his earlier Breton pictures in having a markedly exotic character; the sober colours of the Breton countryside are now replaced by gorgeous harmonies.

Plate xxxv. *Nave Nave Mahana* (Days of Delight),

1896. 37⅜ × 51⅛ in. (95 × 130 cm.). Musée des Beaux-Arts, Lyon. An idyll of Tahiti, of the grace and dignity of the simple life close to nature. Tall statuesque figures set between trees at different intervals in depth forming a complex but harmonious relationship; every section of the picture plays its part in the design. The viewpoint is that of the spectator on the ground. Instead of the well-defined areas of contrasting colours found in most of the works of 1889 — 91, there is now a more unified tone and each picture has its particular colour key.

The influence of the idylls of Puvis de Chavannes is apparent here, especially in the complex rhythmical design. But whereas Puvis depicted a neo-classical world remote from life, Gauguin's arcadia was founded on his own experience, and hence has a warm and living quality.

Plate xxxvi. *Te Arii Vahine* (Woman with Mangoes), 1896. 38$\frac{3}{16}$ × 51$\frac{3}{16}$ in. (97 × 130 cm.). The Pushkin Museum, Moscow. Sometimes known as 'The King's Wife'. Gauguin made a sketch of this picture in a letter to Monfried of April 1896 and described it as follows: 'I have just made a picture of 130 cm. by 1 metre which I think is even better than anything else to date: a naked queen lying on a green carpet, a servant picking fruit, two old men, near the big tree, discussing the tree of knowledge; a beach in the background . . . I think that in colour I have never before made anything of such a majestic deep sonority. The trees are in flower, the dog is on guard, the two doves on the right are cooing.'

Plate xxxvii. *No Te Aha Oe Riri* (Why are you angry?), 1896. 37⅛ × 51¼ in. (95 × 129.6 cm.). The Art Institute of Chicago, Mr & Mrs Martin A. Ryerson Collection. The composition is unusually spacious for Gauguin. Verticals and horizontals lend measure and dignity to the scene; the scale is set by the human figure.

Plate xxxviii. *Portrait of the Artist (at Golgotha)*, 1896. 29⅞ × 25⅛ in. (76 × 64 cm.). Sao Paulo Museum of Art. Inscribed 'Près du Golgotha'. Almost certainly painted in the latter part of the year, when he was passing through a period of ill-health and profound depression. As in several pictures executed in Brittany in 1889 he has portrayed himself as Christ, accentuating the resemblance by means of a tunic; two weird heads are introduced in the background.

Gauguin, who followed Renan in denying the divinity of Christ, was nevertheless very much interested in parables because of the way they could be used to convey more than one meaning.

Plate xxxix. *Nevermore*, 1897. $23\frac{3}{8} \times 45\frac{5}{8}$ in. ($59.5 \times$ 116 cm.). The Courtauld Institute of Art, London. Painted in February 1897. Like the similar *Manao Tupapau* (The Spirit of the Dead Watches) of 1893 (Coll. Conger Goodyear, New York) this was inspired by an incident which took place during Gauguin's first visit to Tahiti.

Gauguin relates in *Noa Noa* how he returned home one night long after dark to find Tehura lying naked on the bed, petrified by fear of the *tupapaus*, the legendary spirits of the dead who were said to walk by night. Between her sobs she exlaimed: 'Never again leave me alone like this without a light.'

In describing the picture to Daniel de Monfreid, Gauguin wrote: 'I wanted by means of a simple nude to suggest a certain barbaric luxury of ancient times. The whole is drowned in colours which are deliberately sombre and sad . . . For title, Nevermore; not the raven of Edgar Allen Poe, but the bird of the devil that is keeping watch.'

This painting, which Gauguin considered especially successful, was bought from Monfreid in 1898 by the composer Frederick Delius for 500 francs.

Plate xl. *Te Rerioa* (The Dream), 1897. $37\frac{1}{2} \times 51\frac{1}{4}$ in. (95×130 cm.). The Courtauld Institute of Art, London. Painted in March 1897, immediately after *Nevermore*. *Te Rerioa* (The Dream), he told Monfreid, 'that is the title. Everything is dream-like in this picture; is it the child, is it the mother, is it the horseman on the track or better still is it the dream of the painter!!! All that has nothing to do with painting, people will say. Perhaps, but perhaps not.'

The composition may have been partly inspired by Delacroix's famous picture *Algerian Women*, in which there are two squatting women similarly disposed in the corner of a room. But there is considerable difference between Delacroix's more exotic treatment and these serene, monumental, almost classical figures.

Plate xli. *D'Où Venons Nous? Que Sommes Nous? Où Allons Nous?* (Whence do we come? What are we? Where are we going?), 1897. $54\frac{3}{4} \times 147\frac{1}{2}$ in. (139×374.5 cm.). The Museum of Fine Arts, Boston. Gauguin painted this picture before attempting to commit suicide in January 1898. 'I wanted before dying to paint a large picture which I had in mind, and for the whole month I worked at it day and night in an incredible fever. Lord knows it isn't a painting done like a Puvis de Chavannes, studies from nature, then preparatory cartoon, etc. It was painted without a model,

straight from the brush, on a sackcloth canvas full of knots and wrinkles, so its appearance is terribly rough.

'People will say that it is careless . . . unfinished. It is true that it is difficult to judge one's own work, but nevertheless I believe that this canvas not only surpasses in value all the previous ones, but that I shall never make a better or a similar one. I have put into it before dying all my energy, a passion so painful in terrible circumstances, and a vision so clear, needing no corrections, that the hastiness disappears and life surges up.'

D'Où Venons Nous?, painted as his final statement, a last great picture, not only sums up and to some extent synthesises the various themes which had been preoccupying him, but makes use of actual figures and motifs drawn from earlier pictures. For example, the two shadowy figures by the tree of knowledge were derived from *Te Arii Vahine* (Plate xxxvi); the old woman on the left appears in many earlier works, including *Soyez amoureuses et vous serez heureuses* of 1889 (p. 20); the child eating a fruit resembles a child in *Nave Nave Mahana* (Plate xxxv); the two squatting women who look towards us are sisters of those in *Nafea Foa Ipoipo* (Plate xxxi); and the girl on the left, leaning on one hand, together with the strange bird beside her, are drawn from *Vairumati* of 1897 (Musée du Louvre).

Plate xlii. *The White Horse*, 1898. $55\frac{1}{2} \times 36$ in. (141×91 cm.). Musée du Louvre, Paris. Presumably painted between January 1898 and April, when he was forced to take a clerical job in Papeete and had to give up painting until the end of the year. Its sombre colours, and in particular its large areas of ultramarine, relate it to *D'Où Venons Nous?* One of the most poetic and mysterious of Gauguin's paintings.

Plate xliii. *Faa Iheihe* (Decoration), 1898. $21\frac{1}{4} \times 66\frac{3}{4}$ in. (54×169.5 cm.). Reproduced by courtesy of the Trustees of the Tate Gallery, London. Painted about the same time as *The White Horse*, though possibly the later of the two; the horseman on the right appears in both pictures. Its format resembles that of *D'Où Venons Nous?*, but unlike the latter it has no definite symbolic content. The mellow, golden colours and the references to a pastoral life amid fruit and flowers reflect Gauguin's reviving health and peace of mind.

The influence of Javanese sculptured friezes appears not only in the frieze-like conception, but in the attitude of certain figures such as the woman in the centre with the palm of her hand raised between her breasts. At the same time, there are echoes of Puvis de Chavannes and even of the Parthenon frieze.

Plate xliv. *Three Tahitians*, 1899 (?). 28 × 36¾ in. (71.5 × 93 cm.). The National Gallery of Scotland, Edinburgh. The date on this picture seems to be '99' (i. e. 1899), but has sometimes been read as '97' (1897). The two outer figures appear again, full-length, against a similar background, in a composition called *Maternity* which exists in two versions: Coll. Mr & Mrs David Rockefeller, New York (undated, but probably c. 1896) and the Pushkin Museum, Moscow (dated 1899). This picture is slightly closer to the latter. It is quite common for Gauguin to use more or less the same figures several times over in different combinations.

Plate xlv. *Still Life with the Painting 'Hope' by Puvis de Chavannes*, 1901. 25¾ × 30¼ in. (65.5 × 77 cm.). Nathan Cummings Collection, Chicago. Gauguin asked Monfreid to send him some flower seeds, and in April 1899 was able to report that most of the plants had reached maturity and were flowering marvellously. In 1901 he painted four or five still lifes, all of sunflowers, clearly with van Gogh's sunflower paintings in mind. As van Gogh said: 'Gauguin . . . has a perfect infatuation for my sunflowers.'

The picture at the upper left is a representation of a study by Puvis de Chavannes in the Louvre, of which Gauguin had a photograph in his hut; the smaller picture is by Degas.

Plate xlvi. *Contes Barbares* (Barbaric Tales), 1902. 51⅛ × 36 in. (130 × 91.5 cm.). Folkwang Museum, Essen.

Like the two following works, this was painted after Gauguin's move to the Marquesas Islands. 'I am more and more pleased with my decision', Gauguin told Monfreid in November 1901, 'and I assure you that from the point of view of painting, this is *Admirable*. Models!!! a marvel . . . Here poetry emerges of its own accord and it is enough to let oneself dream in painting to suggest it.'

The devil-like figure on the left was based on Gauguin's portraits of Meyer de Haan made in 1889; the girl on the right seems a little reminiscent of Botticelli.

Plate xlvii. *Riders on the Beach*, 1902. 25¾ × 29⅞ in. (65.5 × 76 cm.). Folkwang Museum, Essen. Gauguin painted in 1902 two pictures of riders on the beach near Atuana; the other picture, with more figures, is in the Niarchos Collection. They seem to have been inspired partly by memories of Degas's paintings of race-course scenes.

Plate xlviii. *L'Appel* (The Call), 1902. 51¼ × 35½ in. (130 × 89.5 cm.). The Cleveland Museum of Art, Gift of Hanna Fund and Leonard C. Hanna, Jr. Despite his failing health, Gauguin was able on the Marquesas Islands to paint several masterpieces. This picture exemplifies as well as any the form of art for which he was striving: evocative content ('In painting, one must search rather for suggestion that for description, as is done in music') and extremely lyrical and 'musical' colours.

The pose of the figure with upraised arm was derived from the Parthenon frieze.